EARTH ANGELS
ARE EVERYWHERE
ARE YOU ONE?

D1080893

To John, Adrian and Claire, three Earth Angels who
bring great joy to my life.

EARTH ANGELS ARE EVERYWHERE ARE YOU ONE?
Dolores Keaveney

Published by Dbee Press,
8 New Row, Belvedere, Mullingar, Co. Westmeath, Ireland.

Design and print by Mind's i Graphic Design Limited,
23 Marlinstown Park, Mullingar, Co. Westmeath, Ireland.
www.mindsi.ie

Editor: Aoife Barrett

ISBN: 978-0-9562616-4-9

Written and Illustrated by Dolores Keaveney
Email: d_keaveney@yahoo.co.uk
www.doloreskeaveney.com

Earth Angels
are everywhere
are you one?

POEMS & GUIDANCE FOR AN EARTH ANGEL

DOLORES KEAVENEY AUTHOR & ILLUSTRATOR

PUBLISHED BY DBEE PRESS 2011

Joyful Earth Angels are always near,

To give words of encouragement and good cheer,

To someone who feels a little bit down,

We put a smile on their face and remove their frown.

Make a difference today. If there is something you can do to help someone, do not hesitate – put it into action.

Miracles happen when people are touched by love.

"A gentle word, a kind look, a good-natured smile can work wonders and accomplish miracles."

William Hazlitt (1778 – 1830)

Teachers are Earth Angels working each day,

Teaching our children how to live in a good way,

No fighting, no bullying, just how to begin,

To give to each other that love from within.

Patience, kindness, gentleness and love are the only way.

"The greatest happiness of life is the conviction that we are loved; loved for ourselves, or rather, loved in spite of ourselves."

Victor Hugo (1802 – 1885)

Earth Angels sit and spend many hours,

Sending good thoughts to this planet of ours,

Our planet needs healing in the most urgent way,

That's why Earth Angels send out our love every day.

Take a moment today, radiate love in all directions throughout the Universe to all beings on our planet – wish everyone well.

"Of all the Gods, Love is the best friend of humankind, the helper and healer of all ills that stand in the way of human happiness."

Plato (427 – 347 BC)

Earth Angels in hospitals work day and night,

Dark days of sickness transformed into light,

We were given this gift from Heaven above,

To care and look after each patient with love.

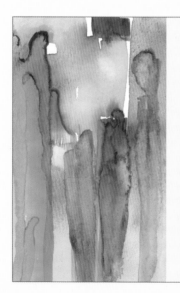

Have you time to visit the sick today or maybe to drop in to see someone living alone or your neighbour?

"No act of kindness, no matter how small, is ever wasted."

Aesop (620 – 560 BC)

Earth Angels listen with the greatest of care,

To a person living in grief and despair,

We comfort this person with love and
a prayer,

Letting them know we will always be there.

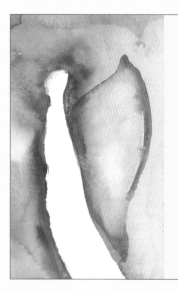

Earth Angels bring hope to people in despair.

Maybe you can too?

"There is no medicine like hope, no incentive so great, and no tonic so powerful as expectation of something tomorrow."

Orison Swett Marden (1850 – 1881)

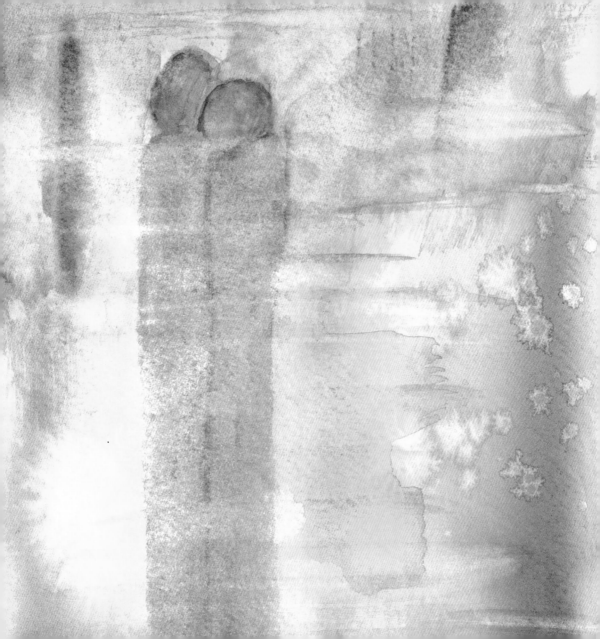

Looking after a child is an Earth Angel's gift,

For a mother and father, what a joy, what a lift.

Through the ups and the downs,
the troubles and strife,

We bring joy, peace and love to its life.

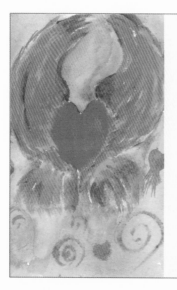

A hungry child needs feeding today.

"For I was hungry and you gave me food, I was thirsty and you gave me drink, I was a stranger and you welcomed me, I was naked and you clothed me, I was sick and you visited me, I was in prison and you came to me."

Matthew (25.35 – 40 ESV)

Earth Angels are here, no doubt about that,

When friends are lonely and in need of a chat,

They can tell us their troubles while we sit and listen,

That's an Earth Angel's calling, an Earth Angel's mission.

One of the best ways to help someone is to listen with love. Make this your mission today.

"We are all born for love. It is the principle of existence, and its only end."

Benjamin Disraeli (1804 – 1881)

Earth Angels generously give to the homeless,

Lying there on the street with their lives
in a mess,

No warm home to go to, no nice meal to eat,

Just a cold lonely pavement, they could do
with a treat.

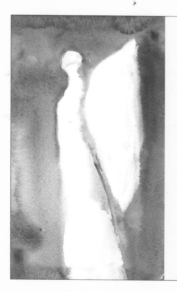

*An Earth Angel would work
for the good of others, as well as
themselves. Would you?*

---

*"It is one of the most beautiful compensations
of this life that no man can sincerely try to help
another without helping himself."*

     Ralph Waldo Emerson (1803 – 1882)

1023, 829 | 202·15
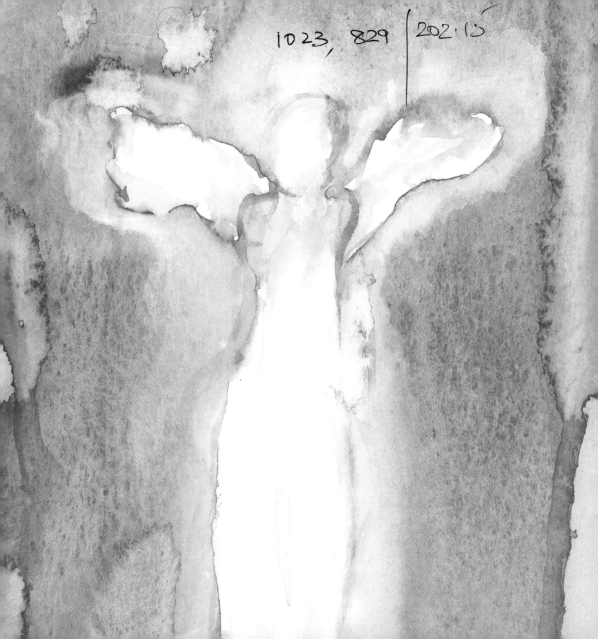

Earth Angels help and support the forlorn,

In a far distant land, so ravaged and torn,

Make a difference, change a life, is our call loud and clear,

Free them from hopelessness, poverty and fear.

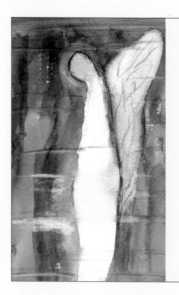

Think of the people suffering because of famine or war throughout the world. Then make a conscious decision to give generously today – because in giving you receive.

"Do all the good you can, by all the means you can, in all the ways you can, in all the places you can, at all the times you can, to all the people you can, as long as ever you can."

John Wesley (1703 – 1791)

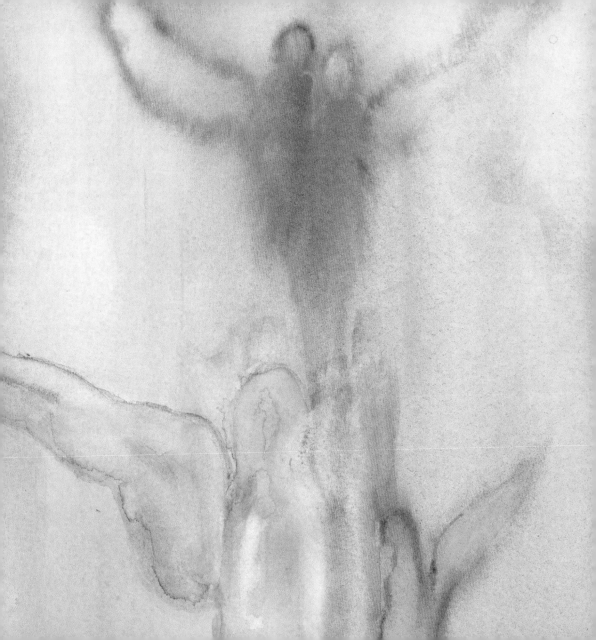

Earth Angels help all the people they meet,

Family, friends, the man in the street,

The hungry and lonely, the rich and the poor,

All Earth Angels do this, that's one thing for sure.

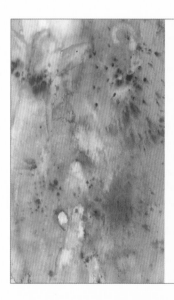

Have you been putting off connecting with someone – a friend, a mother, a son or a daughter? Take time today to get in touch.

"Let us be grateful to people who make us happy, they are the charming gardeners who make our souls blossom."

Marcel Proust (1871 – 1922)

Earth Angels devote their lives every day,

To the elderly in such a loving way,

Helping them to live with dignity before that call from above,

To move on to their next life, full of joy, hope and love.

Respect the life experience of the elderly and gain wisdom from them.

"Grow old along with me! The best is yet to be, the last of life, for which the first was made."

Robert Browning (1812 – 1889)

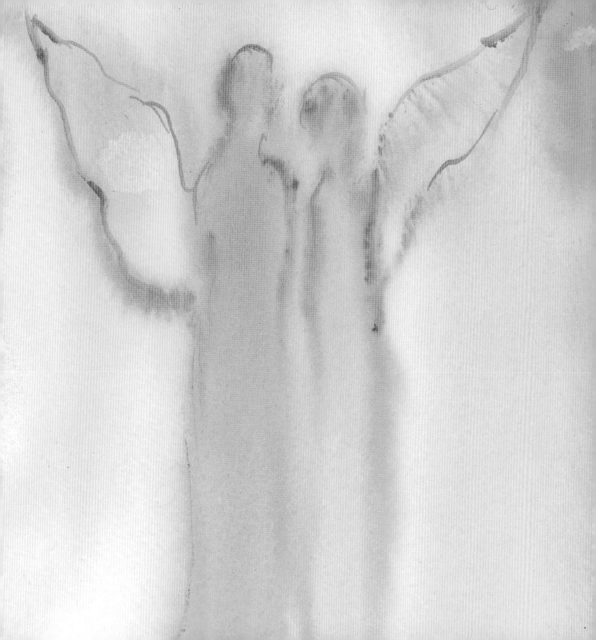

An Earth Angel's presence consoles
the bereaved,

Just a kind word, a gesture, a genuine deed,

A shoulder to lean on, when all hope is lost,

Giving with love, never counting the cost.

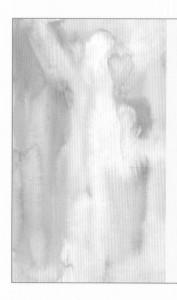

*A small act of loving kindness will
bring joy to a lonely heart today.*

*"Kindness is the language, which the deaf can
hear and the blind can see."*

Mark Twain (1835 – 1910)

Earth Angels everywhere show kindness to all,
A word of thanks, a small phone call,
A helping hand, when needed most,
A listening ear when all seems lost.

We do those things, because you see.
We are Earth Angels – You and Me.

Sometimes we have a tendency to be hard on ourselves.
Today remind yourself that you are as worthy of love as others.
Begin to love yourself more today.

"You, yourself, as much as anybody in the entire universe, deserve your love and affection."
Buddha (563 – 483 BC)

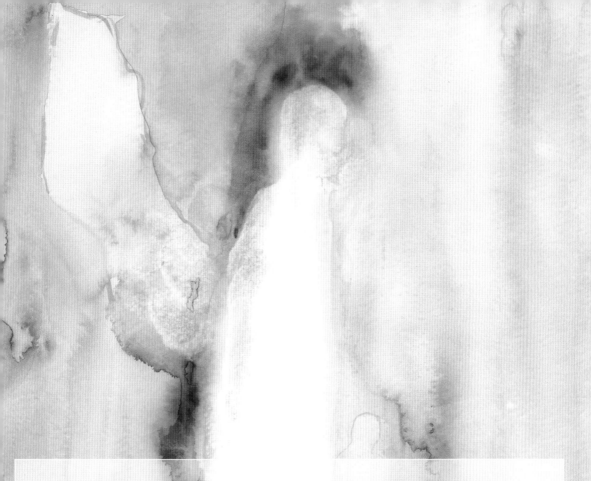

PEACE – PEACE – PEACE
Bring peace to a situation now.

"Peace and friendship with all mankind is our wisest policy, and I wish we may be permitted to pursue it."

Thomas Jefferson (1743 – 1826)

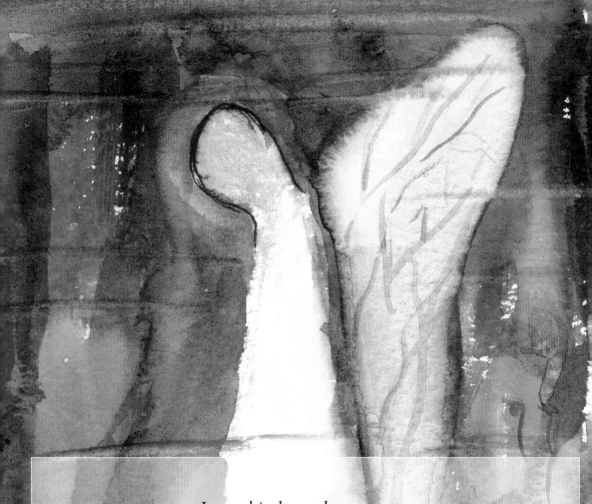

Just a kind word, a gesture.

"*Keep it true, keep it simple and watch your joy grow.*"
Lucinda Drayton

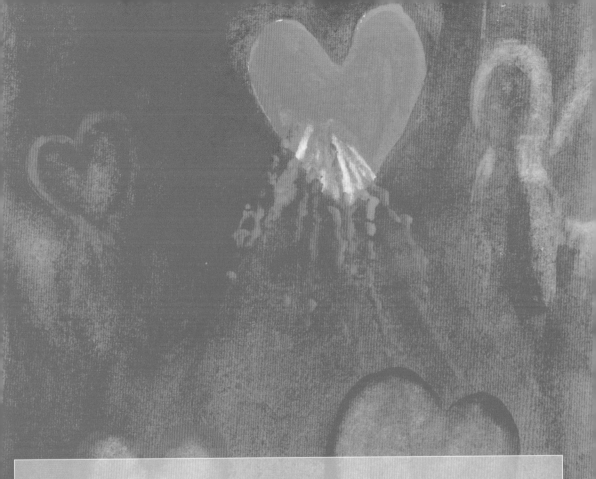

Is there someone you feel anger, resentment and bitterness towards? It is now time to start the healing process. Start today.

"Never does the human soul appear so strong as when it foregoes revenge and dares to forgive an injury."

Pastor Edwin Hubbel Chapin (1814 – 1880)

It is possible for us to have a loving heart.
Heal your heart today through the power of loving kindness
and compassion.

Earth Angels are everywhere;
are you one?

Acknowledgements:

I would like to express my heartfelt gratitude to the many people who have helped me with this book:

My family for their loving support as always.

Cormac Finnery and Margarita Stephens of Mind's i Graphic Design for their invaluable help and expertise in the production of this book.

Aoife Barrett of Barrett Editing for her patience and encouragement.

Lucinda Drayton, Maria Bourke, Patricia Sheehan and Kathleen Walsh for their beautiful endorsements and all the Earth Angels who help and inspire me daily.

I wish to acknowledge the people whose quotations I have used in this book. No matter how ancient the quotations are they inspire the world.

And finally a big thanks to my husband John for everything.